To: Virginia,
Best Wishes —
Alyce Lunsford

IN
TOUCH

Alyce Lunsford

Winston-Derek Publishers, Inc.
Pennywell Drive—Post Office Box 90883
Nashville, Tennessee 37209

Copyright © 1988 by Winston-Derek Publishers, Inc.

All rights reserved. No part of this book may be reproduced in any form without written permission from the publishers, except by a reviewer who may quote brief passages in a review to be printed in a newspaper or magazine.

First printing

PUBLISHED BY WINSTON-DEREK PUBLISHERS, INC.
Nashville, Tennessee 37205

Library of Congress Catalog Card No: 87-51043
ISBN 1-55523-81-9

Printed in the United States of America

CONTENTS

Address Unknown	1
Sunday Afternoon	2
Thank You for Not Smoking	3
The New Arrival	4
Amen	5
The Injustice	6
Kinship	8
That Dog's Outside	9
The Prelude	10
New Grave	11
The Brave One	12
First Snowfall	13
A Path of Love	14
Nice Little Girls	15
Self-Taught	16
October 21	17
A Need for Color	18
The Short Cake	19
Visitor's Day	20
Spring Sign	22
If I Am Right	23
The Cookbook Says	24
Katie's Time	25
These Days	26
The Team	27
My Sister's Child	28
Mariah's Choice	29
Telling the News	32
The Encounter	33
The Quiet Is So Loud	34
Legacy	35
Denial	36
The Presents	37

A Collection of Blue	38
Ambition	39
K-Mart Sells Sweaters	40
December	41
Unfinished Projects	42
The First One	43
For Christmas Day	44
The Professional	45
Tables	46
Flu Shot	47
Another Time	48
The Gardener	49
Always On	50
Christmas Past	52
In Touch	53
The Outlets	54
Mature Love	55
Evening Out	56
Martha	58
Place of Business	59
The Preacher's Bride	60
Coming of Age	62
Tying the Knot	63
On Hold	65
Our Girl	66
Is This the Day?	67
One Size Fits All	68
The Aunts	69
A Skinny Can't Relate	71
Change of Life	72
Be My Valentine	74
Thomas at Two Months	75
Jane	76
Annie's Tree	77
Recovery Room	78
Not Your Basic Gardener	79
The Spouse's Tour	80

Bud	81
The Fitting	83
Before the Funeral	84
The Banquet Speaker	85
The Linen Closet	86
The Instructor	87
The Shopping Trip	88
Visiting	89
The Swimming Lesson	90
New Mother	91
Any News?	92
Where Has the Time Gone?	93
Clean Up	94
The Female	95
When I Go	96
Busybody	97
Retirement	98
The Cemetery	99
One Day at a Time	100
When I Am Old	102
Easter Bonnet	103
Brother Ron and Sister Phyllis	104
Nature's Gift	106
Photo	107
Daughters, Finally	108
Old Friend	109
Goodnight	110
September Morning	111
Comfort	112
Day People	113

There is communication and sharing when people are in touch.
When we are really in touch, there is feeling.

This book is dedicated to my sisters who touch my life in a very special way.

ADDRESS UNKNOWN

*Nutrition counselors
Have a plan
To help you lose weight.*

*I joined
Bought leotards
Packaged meals
And kept an appointment
With their size four leader
Paid enough to own the place.*

*Last week they honored me
With a life membership
This morning I found
The building closed.*

*A notice on the window says
Moved out of state
Address unknown.*

SUNDAY AFTERNOON

*A snack for lunch
Then two or three
Delightful hours
Reading the paper.*

*We wink occasionally
Glance up and smile
Love does not need words.*

*The phone doesn't ring.
No one visits
I wish I could bottle this
Lovely afternoon
And pour some of it out
    When things get hectic.*

THANK YOU FOR NOT SMOKING

*Makes me mad
To see their sign
Thanking me in
Advance.*

*Makes me want
To light up
For spite.*

*I'm in favor
of everyone making
A choice
With no suggestion
That your preference
Should be mine.*

THE NEW ARRIVAL

Any day she'll find herself dethroned.
She doesn't want to share anything
Her daddy's lap belongs to her.
The park is one of her favorite places
And she is used to having ice cream on demand.

She thinks a baby will be neat
All powdery and sweet.
Doesn't know they yell and scream and spit up.
She is impatient and has learned to stamp her foot
Has no idea the baby can't play with her on arrival.

"I'm the line-leader," she declares firmly at playschool,
And she volunteers to boss the whole crowd.
She is quick and smart and will teach this baby a thing or two.
As she adjusts to being a big sister, it may be painful to watch.

Someone must be close by to be twice as loving
And to help her through the first few months.
Although she will be shocked that she must share attention,
It won't be long before the new baby will become her very own.

AMEN

*I twirl the channel selector
From one TV preacher to another.
I'd hoped to hear the Word.*

*Instead they beg nonstop
As the lights flash
And the phones ring
To save our stations and satellite
Support our university
Fund the purchase of limousines
    to collect the poor
      for services
And send the group on another
    cruise retreat.*

Hallelujah, I guess.

THE INJUSTICE

*She fried the eggs, mopped the floor and smiled.
She chattered as she memorized sign shapes
And fretted about parallel parking.*

*Her ambition was modest, just to drive to the
    beauty parlor and to church.
At ten o'clock each day she and her instructor
    crept away from the curb
In our old Chevrolet.*

*Mama never drove over 35 and dreaded stoplights
    and intersections.
When they went to get the license she was nervous
    but passed the first time.*

*That night we had a party.
Celebrated with special foods and smiles.
Everyone but Papa.
He was quiet and didn't eat and said,
"We're finished with this driving foolishness;
It's gone too far. You're not to drive again."*

*He left the table, looked straight at Mama and
    slammed the door.
She followed him and also slammed the door.
We passed around the cobbler, but nobody was hungry.
Voices were raised in the next room.
We knew he never refused Mama anything.*

*She had stopped crying when she pulled a suitcase
    off the shelf.
Her eyes were dull and red.
I was afraid she'd leave.
That threat didn't sway him, and there was no compromise.
Days of silence followed.
No more talk of shifting gears and pushing in the clutch.*

It was years after he died before she finally drove.
By then she was weak and old.
Another instructor went with her to get the license,
 but she never knew confidence or pleasure.
I think she felt guilty every time she drove.
She developed cataracts and gave up driving.

This happened a long time ago and was none of my business.
But he had no right....

 he had no right.

KINSHIP

*We entered the bank together.
I held the door as she shuffled through
    wearing reinforced, built-up shoes.
As she placed her deposit on the counter
    I noticed twisted fingers and deformed wrists.
She presented her identification with difficulty,
    but the purse clasp was too hard to close.*

*I wanted to speak to her, to ask questions.
How long have you had arthritis?
How long did this deformity take?
The pain?
How do you manage?
What are the things you've given up?*

*I cannot ask for the facts I wish to know.
I cannot bear to know exactly how this disease
    progressed.
So I adjust my hand splint and shy away.*

*I hold the door for her as we leave.
I smile and say, "Good morning.
Nice day, isn't it?"*

THAT DOG'S OUTSIDE

That dog's outside
It's ten degrees
I'd let him in
But he's got fleas
I think that I
Just heard him sneeze
That dog's outside

He's got a house
And blanket too
I know he's cold
He'll catch the flu
I cannot sleep
It's gonna sleet
That dog's outside

And as I go
To call him in
My son calls down
And says he's been
Beside his bed
All snug he said
That dog's inside

In a day or two
The fleas will mate
I can see it now
They'll incubate
I'll swear again
Not to care again
Put that dog outside!

THE PRELUDE

Our friends are unable to join us
And I am glad.
Four long quiet days.
    And lazy sunlit mornings
    Miles of beach to walk.
    Restful afternoons
    Uninterrupted conversations.

He naps in the hammock.
I read or quilt.
Around us spin circles of renewed affection
    Building and binding
    Restoring our intimacy.

He wakes and reaches for me.
The lap work slides unnoticed
And I am unaware of the ocean's roar.
At dinner we speak of the others
And their arrival in a few days.

Later we walk near the water's edge.
The moon lights his face as he bends and smiles.
At the cottage we toast each other
And enjoy the honeymoon.

I count the precious days remaining
For us to be alone.

NEW GRAVE

*Square blocks of grassy earth
    framed by flowers
        with wasted fragrance.*

*Ribbons wet with rain
    and tears.
We bow beneath the yellow canopy
    in this lonesome place.*

THE BRAVE ONE

I wish someone had pierced my ears when I was two.
I want it done, but I'm afraid.
I make appointments and cancel them.
Do I need more holes in my head?
What about the pain?

As I stand in line for mutilation
A year-old child in front of me barely flinches.
No screams or tears.
I'll be embarrassed if I faint.

My turn?
My stomach lurches.
I sit trembling as they mark the spot.
I cannot see the instrument
But think of a rusty ice pick.

Tiny click-clicks.
That's all?
Gold studs are in?

You mean the suffering I've been through was over nothing?
What a coward.
What a relief.

FIRST SNOWFALL

*The season begins to change
As the leaves swirl.
She used to warn me when a
    storm was expected.*

*She watched the weather carefully.
The first snowfall was her favorite.
She called it a great white blanket
And so it will be for her this year.*

A PATH OF LOVE

Between potting and transplanting he designed
    and built a sloping brick path
For his daughter's wheelchair.
It winds beside the hollyhocks and in
    between the rows of corn.
Now Lori rides with him to check the squash's
    blooms.

They discuss serious subjects like the growth
    of broccoli and the length of watermelon runners,
And whether they need rain.
He asks her to name the blue-green lizard beneath
    the cabbage leaves.
They check the pansy plants, and she points to the
    variety of fern she prefers.

Outside with him each day, Lori is beginning to tan,
    and her nose is sprinkled with freckles.
Her world widens as she rolls her chair along the
    smooth bricks.
She rides close to him as they put out fresh birdseed.
He never hurries as they hold hands and share.

She learns about birds and plants
    and a lot about love.

NICE LITTLE GIRLS

In fourth grade I discovered the telephone.
Every afternoon after school I called boys.
We giggled, compared homework and talked about
    important things.

I had no idea it was not considered nice.
My teacher suggested privately that little girls
    were not supposed to call boys.
"Ever," she said firmly.
David's mother had complained.
She was sure I would like to know that girls
    wait to be called.
Especially nice little girls.

My face burned with embarrassment.
I hated David's mother, my teacher and myself.
My afternoons were long and empty after that,
And it was years before boys rang my telephone.

Who makes up the rules
About what nice little girls can or cannot do?

SELF-TAUGHT

I bought the "Ladies' Complete Sewing Guide"
Studied the pictures
And made a down payment on a sewing machine.
That was twenty years ago
And the ruffler is still in the box.

The instruction book showed no picture
Of facings which do not fit
Or of zippers that droop.
I read about grading seams, clipping curves and
  tailor's tacks.
It took three days just to learn to thread the machine.

I learned to sew straight seams.
Few garments could be completed with straight seams.
There were round armholes and sleeves to coax into place.
"To ease" never meant anything to me
And I grew tired of sleeveless everything.

My sewing machine makes a wonderful desk.

OCTOBER 21

My son phones to say the baby is expected
    in a few hours.
"Probably plenty of time," he speaks quickly.
My heart is pounding, and I put on shoes which
    are not a pair.
I search for my purse and look for keys.

We drive to their town, and I know exactly how
    children feel on Christmas Eve.
We discuss sex and weight, and I bow my head,
    Please God.
We approach the long corridor as our son bursts
    through the swinging doors, both arms raised.
His smile lights up the hall.
"A baby boy, a son, wait till you see him," the
    words tumble out,
"And Julie was . . . is wonderful."

We laugh and weep.
I am drained and aware of God's goodness in a new way.
Our lives are changed.
I wait to see our baby, to introduce myself,
And to promise him everything.

A NEED FOR COLOR

*She called to say that we forgot her lipstick.
"Please remember it when you come to take me home."
We laughed and promised.*

*It was good to hear her voice so strong.
She was homesick, recovering from a heart attack,
    and missing us.
Each day and evening we stayed until visiting hours
    were over
She dreaded hearing that it was time for us to go.*

*It wasn't unusual for her to call to be sure we
    arrived home safely
And to say good night again.
We were preparing her room when the phone rang the
    second time.
"She's not as well," the nurse reported.
"I think you'd better come."*

*We rushed to the hospital and hurried to her floor.
Her doctor's face told us much before he spoke.
"The nurse was arranging her room for the night and
    heard her make a small noise.
There was nothing we could do."*

*I guess we thanked him; I don't know.
He turned to leave as we entered Mother's room.
I felt the tube of lipstick in my pocket and remembered.
I gave it to her nurse, but could not explain
That Mother would want color for her homecoming.*

THE SHORT CAKE

For the first 30 minutes the fluffy
  cake rises.
I peek through the glass in the oven
  door and think,
Nothing to it really.

I ask everyone to walk softly.
I hum a tune and arrange the cooling rack.

Then it defies me, reverses the rising
  process,
Plops in the middle and sags.
Crevices and jagged cracks decorate the top.
The soft cake deflates.

A two-inch short cake,
  a
   g
    a
     i
      n.

VISITOR'S DAY

*He tried to call her while his car was being
    repaired.
She didn't realize it was him and being wary of
    strangers she refused to speak.
Since they chose a nursing home for her, she has
    become fragile and forgetful.
She is thirty miles from him.
They both look forward to the day he visits.*

*He lives at home in two rooms instead of ten.
He misses her, and for six days he is lonely.
On Saturdays they are together from ten till ten.
Everyone welcomes him and watches their tenderness
    in the halls.
They play rummy and take short walks.
He leans on his cane, she on his once strong arm.
Sometimes they whisper and laugh.
She smiles and blushes as she did when she was nineteen.*

*The car was in running shape again.
He whistled as he loaded cupcakes in the backseat.
Because his driver's license was expiring, he went by
    the patrol office.
He had difficulty answering their questions because
    a stroke had slowed his speech.
There was discussion among the examiners about his
    reaction time,
But his hearing was poor so he didn't strain to hear
    details.
He was ready for his license and anxious to visit
    his wife.*

*It had not occurred to him that he wouldn't get
   the license.
They tried to soften the news by suggesting he
   could try again.
The patrolman offered to drive him home, but agreed
   he could drive himself for the last time.*

*He headed towards the busy interstate and kept on
   going.
He sees his wife on visitor's day at ten.*

SPRING SIGN

Little gray buds
Shaped like Q-tips
Appear along the branches
Of the pussy willow
In March.

Each one silently
Announcing
Spring
With a burst of fuzz.

IF I AM RIGHT

*I cannot reason
Why you do not believe in God.
Nor can you imagine why I do.*

*If after death you discover
He does not exist,
Get word to me... whatever it takes,
"I told you so."*

*What message shall I try to send
When I discover in eternity
God lives and always has?*

*There will be no tears in Heaven,
But I shall shed a tiny one for you.*

THE COOKBOOK SAYS

Recipes will be delicious, the cookbook says.
Home economists write glowing descriptions of
    products from their test kitchens.
Luscious photographs inspire the laziest person
    to fold, mix or process.

With all the help they have, everything should be
    perfect.
Their pantry is always stocked
They need no budget,
And they have five hours to make a pie.

They hooked me with a photograph of cucumber salad
    filled with cream and accented with berries.
No problem to assemble; they lead me on.
Just try to unmold it.
I dipped the mold in warm water as directed.
Wonder how many they made before a salad turned
    out whole?

I ran a knife blade around the edges of the mold.
Do I need a challenge such as this?
I wrapped hot towels around it and finally baptized
    it in my sink.
You will hear a tiny thud, the cookbook says, as
    the salad slides onto the platter.

We're having sliced cucumbers for supper tonight.
The garbage men may wonder about the liquid green
    stuff.

KATIE'S TIME

Katie looked after her parents until they died.
By then the man she was interested in didn't come
    around anymore.
She and her brother live together in the homeplace.
He is 74 and crippled with arthritis.

"It isn't safe to leave him.
He doesn't want me to hire anyone; so I try to cope.
My days are all the same.
I prepare him for the day in his wheelchair,
    go to work
    return for lunch
    prepare his supper
    put him to bed.
Sometimes I switch on TV, but I'm so lonesome and
    sorry for my brother, I can't make a decision.
His doctor ordered a rest home.
He doesn't want to go.
I work every day, and all the bills are mine.
I feel that life has left me behind."

As she spoke she twisted a paper napkin until it
    was in shreds.
She bowed her head to hide her tears.
Katie at 55 is alone and burdened with another
    patient's care.

I hug her gently and suggest we go tomorrow to look
    at rest homes
So she can begin to live again,
Before it's too late.

THESE DAYS

The summer that she died
Came and went.
Days too long, too hot.
Days filled with loneliness.

The least thing reminded me
That she was gone.
Seeing her empty chair and open drapes
Gave lonely definition.

Clearing away her personal things
Was one long, tearing gash.
I hurried, thinking how quickly
A wound heals if tended right away.

I was wrong.
Efficiency is ineffective.

THE TEAM

The first time I heard their conversation as
    a customer left the shop,
I thought they were sincere.
"Don't that cut look good on her, Frank?"
Juanita called from her booth in the back.

"You got a real becoming hairdo, Mrs. Willis."
Frank, at the cash register, watched the lady
    sign her check and commented,
"Looks the best ever, Juanita."
Frank didn't bother to look at the customers as
    they left anymore.

The beauty shop is called "Frank's Salon,"
But the business is a husband-wife team.
For twenty years they've been supplying shampoos,
    sets and conversation.
Long ago they decided to compliment every person
    as she left the shop.

They never miss.
"Frank, take a good look at Gladys. Her color job
    is perfect.
Reminds me of I Love Lucy, it's such a pretty red."
As though it were a tennis game, Frank returns the serve,
"Yeah, that henna flame is the finest color red I've
    ever seen."

It isn't.
Gladys looks as if she is wearing a curly red mop.
I'm embarrassed to think she's going out that way.
"Good-bye, pretty," Juanita gets in one more lick.
Gladys looks in the mirror and smiles.

I wish they'd just tell their customers good-bye.

MY SISTER'S CHILD

I picture you sometimes,
Dear stillborn child I never saw.
I know you were there.
I felt you kick
And imagined your smile.

Your mother and I were young that year.
She dreamed of your curls
And blue eyes.
You had both.

When I arrived to greet you,
You were gone.
I still feel an empty place.
The dress made for you had
Tiny roses on the yoke,
And lace.

Now you wear the dress and lie
Beneath a headstone where little
Lambs frolic
On fields of bronze turned green
With age.

MARIAH'S CHOICE

Possessions were few
*   medicines, prescriptions, and some clothes.*
When she entered the nursing home in her wheelchair
*   Mariah was holding a picture in her lap.*
They told her that she could hang it if a nail was
*   already in place.*

In her room there was a single bed, a small table
*   and a dresser.*
She hardly noticed the cloudy, speckled mirror.
A deep brown chair was supported by books which almost
*   steadied it.*
There was one window; it was too high for her to
*   see outside.*

Mariah took an old calendar down and hung
*   her picture in its place.*
"They should be glad I covered such a badly faded spot,"
*   she said aloud.*
Then exhausted, she wheeled to the narrow bed, crawled
*   in and faced the wall.*

Mariah's poor eyesight caused the accident.
She knew the tree roots were near the clothesline.
As she fell she heard her hip crack and realized her
*   moment of carelessness.*
Both her children were out of town, but her neighbors
*   took her to the hospital.*
After her surgery she planned to split the time needed
*   to recuperate between the children.*

*When the children visited, she listened as they spoke
     of problems each would have caring for her.
Perhaps they thought her too sleepy to hear.
They wondered aloud if her hip would mend
And how long it could take.*

*Maggie explained she was busy increasing sales and
     was supposed to entertain clients regularly.
She was not free to take on nursing care.
Bill was traveling now, and his wife had her club meetings.
His kids needed all the bedrooms.
He hoped to add a den one day to gain a little privacy
     for himself.*

"It isn't that we don't want to help, Mother," Maggie began,
"It's a little difficult to drop everything suddenly."
Maggie brushed her mother's hair back on the pillow.
"We'll work something out, but I just don't know what."
Mariah looked her straight in the eye.
"It's all right. I prefer a nursing home."
*They paid no attention to Mariah and continued to list
     their excuses.
She steadied her voice and spoke louder than before.*
"I repeat. I am going to go to a nursing home."

*Bill patted her hand and smiled, happy to be handed a
     solution.
Maggie breathed deeply and relaxed for the first time.*
"If you need anything just have them call me," Bill said
     as his lips brushed her hair.
He picked up his briefcase, waved and left the room.

*Maggie walked to the window, checked her watch and
     realized she was late for her next appointment.*
"Mama, I've got to go, too. I'll be in touch."

Mariah rested after they left and thought about her situation.
It was a relief not to have to smile for them anymore.
She stayed in the hospital for ten days, and the staff helped her find a nursing home.
After she transferred and got settled she said to herself,
"I can take my own time healing this hip.
I'll go home when I'm ready.
I won't have to cheer up anyone else every day
I can watch my programs on TV and turn up the volume loud.
When I'm strong I'm going to look out that window and watch people.
Maybe I'll meet new folks, maybe make some friends.

One thing for sure I'm not a burden to my children.
It feels good to make my own choice."

TELLING THE NEWS

I am not going to inflict a hospital photo of
 a newborn child on anyone.
What can you say about a wrinkled, red person,
 asleep with a number on its chest?
I'm not going to carry a brag-book and bore
 everyone with vital statistics.

I will not force others to listen while I discuss
 the baby's digestive system
Or colicky smiles.
I'm going to forget to tell them about the teething details, and the
 gurgling sounds.

What a lie!
While I'm trying to remain silent about this
 first grandchild
I'll make notes and fill you in on all these
 important events in my Christmas newsletter.

Maybe I'll also call you once a week so you
 won't miss a thing.
I know you can hardly wait.

THE ENCOUNTER

I watched you park, and set your flares.
You walked quickly to both corners of the block.
I felt uneasy, set the back screen lock, and
 continued ironing.
I thought how silly I was to be afraid.

It required little effort to force the flimsy lock.
I heard the screen scrape as you slid it sideways.
You approached me with a sly, suggestive smile.
The iron I threw only made you angry
And there was no one to hear my screams.

I hoped you'd settle for money,
But you didn't have dollars on your mind.

How legitimate your being here would seem to
 those who saw you leave
In your service uniform and company truck.
You drove away as though you had simply checked
 the furnace.
I'll never rid my house of the smell of you.
I have no strength or need for screaming now.

THE QUIET IS SO LOUD

*Now that I don't need the space,
    there is room to spare.
The closets are straight, and there
    is order everywhere.
The cupboard is full of dishes seldom used,
And I no longer save jelly glasses
    covered with Flintstone characters.*

*My large chicken fryer has been replaced
    by a six-inch skillet.
There are no ball team uniforms to wash
    and dry.
I sleep late because the days are long.
No one plays the piano or bounces a
    basketball in the house.
The sofa where the children sprawled looks
    deserted.*

*I watch any TV program I choose.
I like not having to tolerate rock-and-roll.
I do not need to ask that the stereo be
    adjusted.
The morning paper is mine.*

*I'm finding the quiet can be loud and the
    space lonely.
Where was all this silence and room when I
    needed it?*

LEGACY

*I used to wait on the porch watching for Daddy to
 turn the corner.
I played red-light or giant-step.
As soon as I saw him I ran with arms outstretched.
I double-skipped beside him trying to match his stride,
 and I begged to wear his work cap.
He'd grin at me with his wonderful lopsided smile of
 approval.
Inside he'd swing me to the top of the pile of tobacco
 Mama had graded that day.
Then I would pretend to fly as I jumped into his arms
 and giggled.*

*Near our house he kept a cow.
I went with him to milk her every day.
We walked single file through the weeds along a narrow
 path,
That's when I'd find the nickel.
He must have tossed it in front of me as I skipped along.
He said finding one meant good luck.
He declared I must be the luckiest child in the world.*

*He could not let me keep the coin because there were
 bills to pay.
He said that finding the coin was what brought good
 luck.*

*Whenever I have a lucky incident now
I touch the nickel I keep in my pocket.
I thank him and treasure my good luck and memories.*

DENIAL

They expect me to believe one person?
One phone call?
Perhaps I misunderstood.
They probably dialed wrong or have
    reported it incorrectly.
How silly they will feel when they
    get it straight.

They've hung a wreath on the door.
People visit and confirm that she is gone.
They are smothering me.
They do not realize there is a mistake
And they have no real reason to be here.

Any minute she'll probably walk in and say,
"What in the world is going on?"
Then I will laugh and shout,
"See? I told you she was fine."

THE PRESENTS

*The year I learned to print,
I made out my Christmas list,
Placing extravagant gifts
Beside each sister's name.*

*My allowance included
Four dimes, one nickel and six pennies.
Mother and I went shopping,
But magnificent purchases were expensive.
Everything cheap was ordinary.*

*We decided to buy powder puffs,
Three for each girl.
Mother bought yards of lace, and
I pulled a thread to make a ruffle.
I wound the lace around each one.
Mother stitched the edge and helped
    with knots and praise.*

*Each Christmas I think of those simple
Gifts made for sisters I adored.
They smiled and wondered aloud
How I knew exactly what they had
    always wanted.*

A COLLECTION OF BLUE

*I wonder who used the dishes I treasure.
Who washed the bowls and plates and
    polished this scalloped platter?
They are alike in color, but the designs
    are unmatched.
Most of the pieces are ordinary and old.
Some of the cups are chipped, so I handle
    them with extra care.*

*I am pleased to find an odd dish for this
    collection.
A covered tureen, a pitcher found in
    different places.
It isn't required that I set the table
    with them.
It is enough to admire them on open shelves.
I arrange them again and again, admire their
    variety and color
And enjoy a link with the past.*

AMBITION

"What will you be when you grow up?"
Mother answered for me, "A nurse."
She was proud when I entered training in the fall.

"I love the uniform," she'd say
And she gave me a watch and white shoes.
She fingered the lining of my cape
And told her friends I was doing well.

I studied and worked and liked none of it.
People die in hospitals!
Does she know?
How could she want me here?
I bathed patients on Christmas Day and New Year's
While my friends were home celebrating.

I filled out forms, admitted patients, and
    stabbed their veins for blood.
I tried to act detached.
"You're so lucky to be helping sick people,"
    Mother encouraged me
As I complained and grew more miserable every day.

I never got used to festering wounds
And amputated limbs.
Or to her disappointment when I resigned.
She never understood it was she who should have
    trained to comfort fever
And become what she always wanted to be.

K-Mart Sells Sweaters

*If you want a new sweater
I suggest you go buy one
Forget about learning to knit
Don't get hooked on the yarn
Leave the patterns alone
Casting on will give you a fit.*

*The supplies will cost more
Than two sweaters are worth
They never have your pattern size
The needles won't work
Knitting makes your head hurt
You won't knit or purl if you're wise.*

*I tried it once
And once is enough
Ribbing was really a pain
I was doing all right
Just dropped one little stitch
But when the phone rang
I dropped it again.*

*Instead of a sweater
I now have a headband
It's got a few holes
Nevermind
The sweaters at K-Mart
All fit, ready-made
And they're open from 9 until 9.*

DECEMBER

*Nine years ago this Christmas Eve
     you died.
I still think of phoning you to
     ask advice
Or to share a joke I think you'd like.
I can't forget when our days were
     filled with fun.*

*You stopped talking after we knew you
     would leave.
We'd always spoken easily of anything
     that came to mind.
I searched your face for answers and
     reassurance
But you had no answers, and you turned away.*

*Watching you divide your things into
     piles for others seemed unreal.
You boxed and tied in silence.
I brought you news and conversation
It didn't matter; already you were gone.*

*We sat and rocked away those last winter
     afternoons.
Now in the same chair I cradle your
     grandchild
And mine.
The rockers squeak as they did those
     silent days
When we said good-bye.*

UNFINISHED PROJECTS

Teach yourself to crochet?
With hook and yarn you make the same monotonous
*   stitch over and over.*

Smocking is so beautiful.
Pleat, embroider
Then you must make a garment to show it off.

Anyone can learn to knit,
Purl, or drop a stitch.

Quilt like Grandmother did.
Patch, piece, make smaller stitches with sorer
*   fingers.*

Tie & Dye?
Bleach, tie with string, paint dye on.
What a mess.

There are a few projects I will not complete.
Not even to avoid a guilty feeling.

THE FIRST ONE

My children sneaked in the announcement casually
I wondered if I really heard they expected a baby.

They enjoyed my double take
And laughed at my surprise and tears of joy.
I have not been so happy in a long time.

They are ready to welcome a child
    and so am I.
My concentration is poor.
I can think of nothing else.

I find myself gazing out the window
Smiling at the thought.
I think of smocked pinafores with taffeta sashes.
I plan birthday parties and think of sailor suits.
There will be hobbyhorses and sandboxes
And Christmas trees and first rides in the snow.

They will be good parents.
Responsible for sniffles, shots and behavior.
I'll tell him about the old days, spoil a little
    and love a lot.

FOR CHRISTMAS DAY

I am planning a special stocking
    for the new grandchild.
It will hang at the end of the row
    of six stockings,
Filling in the space that has been
    waiting for him.

I'll embroider holly and berries
And drums and rocking horses with
    bright scarves around their necks.
"Thomas" will be stitched on a white
    velvet cuff,
And there will be a shiny silver bell
    on the toe.

This stocking will be red, bright red,
To announce in a crimson shout...
This is my grandson's first Christmas Day!

THE PROFESSIONAL

*I'm tired of waiting tables and
    answering stupid questions.
"Tell me about your ribs," he winks
    and says.
(They hurt; I want to answer.)
"Are they tasty?"
"Our specialty," I reply.*

*I'm sick of smiling.
It wouldn't be so bad to listen
    to customers babble
If I could write down potatoes,
    soup or salad
Without conversation or a phony
    grin.*

*You think the tips are good?
Four booths full of people might
    leave eight quarters.
That's sixteen orders to record,
    deliver and serve with a smile.
I pocket whatever they leave; but
    trays are heavy.
They get a real bargain in me.*

*I love the guy who asks,
"What time do you get off?
I'll show you a good time."
I decline, knowing he's a jerk.
I'm thinking of soaking my feet later
And wiping off this smile.*

TABLES

*At first we used a card table.
We stored it behind a door, then
    unfolded it for two.
We laughed about the rickety leg
    and propped it up with books.*

*Later I found an old pine table.
I bought it for $2.50, refinished it
    and have it still.
It was just the right height for the
    baby's high chair.*

*When the boys came we had a large oak
    table.
It held birthday cakes and pizza for
    friends.
There was plenty of room for making
    model airplanes and for studying.*

*Now I have my mother's walnut table.
She used it 40 years, and it shows her
    loving care.
There wasn't room for it in her small
    apartment.
She used to stroke it as she passed
    through my kitchen, loving it still.
Glad it was used and cherished.*

It's a perfect size for the two of us now.

FLU SHOT

I should get a refund.
First flu shot for me.
I now have the worst cold
I've ever had.

I ache all over.
Eyelashes hurt.
Head feels huge; nose is red.
Look like a frog and sound worse.

The shot was cheap and painless,
(Almost)
I felt so smug and immune.
Is it possible I made an appointment
Paid the bill
And received the flu?

ANOTHER TIME

I learned to spell fudge when
Big sisters spelled one letter at a time
And hurried off to the kitchen to stir cocoa
     and sugar.
They thought I didn't know what was going on.
I remember how good the candy smelled
And how they whispered and giggled and saved
     the pan for me to scrape.

I'd like to spend an afternoon at play
Spreading a napkin and paper cups for a feast.
I'd serve wild strawberries for dessert
To imaginary playmates again.

I'd like to feel the damp curls on my shoulders
Drying in the sun.
Mama wound my hair around her finger and
When she was through, she kissed me every time.

I received a piano for my tenth birthday.
Mama made payments for years, and I skipped to
     music lessons on Saturday.
I like recitals, and although I once forgot
     the song I was supposed to play,
Mama kept smiling and said she was so proud of me.

I rushed to grow up so quickly.
I wanted to wear nail polish and high-heeled shoes
     and to be as grown-up as my big sisters.
Sometimes the little girl in me is difficult to
     remember.

THE GARDENER

You should see his face as he talks about
    his ripening tomatoes.
"They're as thick as grapes and big as your fist."
No weeds are tolerated in his garden,
A tender plant need lots of room to grow,
He tells me how much corn a row should produce.

He likes to crumble the loose black soil
And sift it through his fingers.
He brings tiny plants from his greenhouse
And scoops a hole for each one.

I watch him gently pat the earth, settling them,
And watering with great care.
He protects against insects and harsh weather
And I saw him once rush to cover plants from hail
Without stopping to get his hat.

He is shy, and since we have become friends, I have
    done most of the talking.
He lets me know that he thinks I am special by
    sharing prizes from the garden.
Last Christmas he presented me with a large
    lemon from a plant he nursed for three years.
Around the stem he had tied red ribbons and on the
    homemade card he printed "with love."
I'm going to save that card forever.

ALWAYS ON

Don was a teacher when they married.
After he decided to become a minister, Helen
    tried to be a good wife.

She sang in the choir and substituted for the organist.
Bible study groups met at her home, and she prepared
    refreshments.
She was expected to supervise Girl Scout programs
    and to preside at Circle meetings.

The congregation enjoyed the flowers she brought to
    church.
They took it for granted she would plant, cultivate
    and donate all the floral arrangements.
Her cheesecakes became famous at the Charity Bazaar,
And the young people wanted her to direct their
    weddings and receptions,
And entertain for them, of course.

If she dressed fashionably, she was thought extravagant.
When she wore casual clothes, they did not approve.
She was criticized for taking a part-time job, and the
    people whispered that she neglected her family.
When she was at home full-time, many considered her lazy.

Helen tried to please everyone for ten years.
She had no friends to confide in, and her temper grew
    short.
She smiled and accepted responsibility until last
    Wednesday night.
At choir practice she overheard the ladies saying
    that she had no business wearing a sun-suit
    on her patio.
"You'd think she'd have a little modesty," they gossiped.

*They found her in the church kitchen crying
	hysterically,
"I cannot do this anymore . . . I will not," she screamed.
The doctor ordered complete rest.*

*The women of the church wonder how anyone with so
	much leisure
Could be ordered to do nothing.
They call at the parsonage to be sure she remembers
	it's her turn to fix communion.
They've postponed the revival until she is able to
	entertain the visiting minister and his wife.*

CHRISTMAS PAST

*Each year there were cowboy suits, bicycles and
    basketballs under the tree,*
*And three little boys anxious to find boots and
    football games.*
*They went early in December with their daddy to
    choose a red poinsettia for me.*
Then the festive feeling began.

*Baking began early, and the boys were always hungry
    for cookies and candy.*
*They took turns scraping the pan to get the last
    spoonful.*

*Handmade gifts and presents bought with allowances
    were hidden away.*
*The front door was decorated with santas or snowmen
    made at school.*
Tom drew a face on the gold angel we used on the treetop.
We have used it for 25 years, and I treasure it still.

All the boys were in pageants, plays and choirs.
*They wore old bathrobes and stood as shepherds near
    the manger scene at church.*
*Once we had two kings in the Christmas play, dressed in
    purple and scarlet robes*
And wearing gold foil crowns on top of crew cuts.
One sat down halfway through the play and explained,
"I'm tired from traveling so far from the East."

Today I am sorting snapshots of the family.
There is a special Christmas sparkle in our eyes.
*My sons all are taller than the mantle which still
    holds their stockings,*
And a new grandson will join us this year.
Each Christmas past was better than the one before,
But this one will be the best of all.

IN TOUCH

We fill the inner space meaninglessly.
Ignoring a need to know ourselves
We engage in continuous chatter
        constant motion
         ceaseless activity
Anything to keep from being alone.

We recognize a need for solitude.
There are places inside which seem strange.
Many familiar warts we recognize.
We view many characteristics with disapproval.
Most have escaped notice too long,
And it is painful to look too closely.

Be kind as the space is searched.
Go past facade and detour the impression
    created for others.
Good qualities discovered are worth giving
    without inviting debt,
Or making opportunity for recognition or
    applause.

The world is divided into givers and takers,
    winners and losers.
In touch, we may find exactly who we are.

THE OUTLETS

They pile off the bus,
And they're hunting for bargains
They're all wearing comfortable shoes.
They fan out with tote bags
In every direction
Hurry, there's no time to lose.

They plow through the stacks
Of wicker and linen
Silk flowers, crystal and string.
They settle for split seams
And holes in the knits
At home they would buy no such thing.

They cannot exchange
The things that they buy
They live 200 miles from this lot.
But call it an "Outlet"
And everyone's pleased
With the imported bargains they got.

MATURE LOVE

*Young love was truly special.
Finding a mate was exciting,
And the passion was beautiful.*

*There was a difficult learning stage.
It took time to learn to give, take, share,
Overlook mistakes, communicate, give approval.*

*After thirty years these insecurities are gone.
We are past pettiness and critical judgement.
Ribbons of love, familiarity and desire tie us.
Blows which would have wounded one of us alone
Have bound us more closely.*

*Our love has matured.
There is a dear companionship.
We've shared thousands of meals and years of
    conversation.
We have been blessed with the responsibility of
    children
And the happiness of a family.*

*Jokes and laughter have eased us past monotony.
Often we have the same thoughts at the same time.
We've grown more caring.
We treasure complete trust.
Young love was wonderful, and the first years
    were fun,
But mature love is best of all.*

EVENING OUT

Celebrating Glennis' birthday had worn Ervin out
    for years.
She liked parties, music and activity.
He preferred quiet evenings, TV and staying at home.

This year they had a quiet dinner at a restaurant.
As they were leaving, Glennis heard music playing
    in the lounge.
"Let's stop a minute, honey.
Maybe you'd like a beer?"
Ervin wanted to go home and watch the ballgame on TV,
    but he reluctantly agreed.

Glennis sat down at a small table and smoothed her
    new sequin blouse.
She tapped her toes to the rhythm and drummed her
    fingers on the edge of the table.
"Isn't that the best music, Ervin?"
He didn't answer, but soon relaxed and became drowsy.
Glennis tried not to notice he was bored.
She turned her attention to the dancers whirling by.

She was surprised when a man approached and asked
    if she would care to dance.
"Me?" she turned to see to whom he was speaking.
"Are you talking to me?"
No one had asked her to dance in 25 years.
"Why yes," she glanced at Ervin who was asleep,
"I would like to dance."
They walked to the middle of the floor and danced
    for over an hour.

*The music was wonderful and she followed him
    perfectly.
They returned to the table occasionally, and Ervin
    was still asleep.
At ten o'clock they said good-bye.
Glennis shook Ervin awake.*

*He complained about a crick in his neck and about
    the warm beer.
His complaints didn't bother Glennis.
She picked up her purse, still thinking of the
    fun of the last hour.
"It's nice to see you smile," Ervin said.
"I hope you had a happy birthday.
Want to dance a little?"*

*"Oh no," Glennis was surprised he asked.
Their last dance was at their wedding reception,
"But thank you. I'm much too tired now."
She suddenly remembered she had not asked her
    dancing partner's name.
It didn't matter.
She would never forget him or this evening.
"We'll come back next year and dance," she said,
    hoping to see the same man again.*

MARTHA

*Martha is one who gives with both hands and
     with her heart.
Not small gifts or last minute kindnesses,
But treasures of her time and true concern.*

*It feels comfortable to know her well.
I can trust her with any confidence.
I like her soft blue eyes and the sound of her
     voice.
I love her sense of humor.*

*It pleases me that she never changes.
There is no pretense.
She makes no gestures to impress.
With her I feel at home
And the visit is never long enough.*

*I like knowing she thinks of me when she sees
     a water color
Or reads a poem,
Or hears a funny joke.
I like seeing my pantry shelves crowded with watermelon
     rind pickle she has preserved for me.
I'm not going to live long enough to forget her.
And stop loving her?
I wouldn't know how.*

PLACE OF BUSINESS

My father worked in the basement of our home.
He stood beside a small window coated with fumes
    from flame and solder.
The window was usually open but ventilation was poor.
The basement was lined with brick, and it was cold and
    damp.
I never heard him complain.

He loved his work.
He was an expert with his torch.
With pride he melted silver seams to seal cracked
    metal spots.
Customers watched him repair and restore,
And he often worked twelve-hour days.
During fall and winter he worked many nights.
I heard him whistling sometimes as I fell asleep.

At suppertime Mama opened the basement door and
    called him,
And flapped the fumes with her apron.
When he finally came to the table, he was exhausted.
Often he'd fall asleep with his head in his hands.
Mama didn't disturb him, but quietly began to clean
    the kitchen.
After he rested she took his warm plate from the
    oven and served it with a smile.

THE PREACHER'S BRIDE

When the circuit preacher visited,
It was customary to cover the bed with the best quilt.
Brother Clapp, a bachelor, paid no attention to quilts.
All he required was a feather bed, a platter of fried
     chicken
And four uninterrupted hours to preach on Sundays.

When he married Caroline, the congregation expected
     to have her visit on special occasions
Perhaps for weddings and funerals.
Instead they had to entertain her every weekend.
She never missed a visit.

Housing a bachelor was easy, but having to prepare for
     his wife was an imposition.
The ladies did extra baking and cleaning
And soon grew tired of her regular visits.

Caroline Clapp thrived on the attention and service,
     and she loved the food.
She enjoyed sleeping late snuggled under the handmade
     quilts.
Effie Rountree, a deacon's wife, called the ladies'
     group together
To see if anyone else was as tired of company as she was.

They were.
Effie said, "Put up your best quilt.
Serve her plain vittles, and let her wait on herself."

The next time Caroline arrived, she had to pump her
 own bath water.
They showed her the broom and a porch that needed
 sweeping.
She was told to set the table.
After supper she carried her own plate to the sink.

Brother Clapp was busy preparing his sermon,
He didn't notice Caroline flouncing around
 and poking out her lips.

He could not understand why she decided not to travel
 with him anymore,
Or why she suddenly developed a dislike for quilts of
 any kind.

COMING OF AGE

Vicey, eight years old on Saturday, went to work
    in the big house on Sunday.
She was expected to take her place in the dining room
    as all black girls did who lived on the property.

Rena, her mama, gave Vicey instructions as they neared
    the back porch.
She smoothed Vicey's apron and brushed back her hair.
"Now, honey, smile.
Speak if you're spoken to.
Don't cough or laugh, no matter what you hear.
If you fetch something from the kitchen for them, be
    quick about it."
Vicey looked at her mama and wondered why she was so
    nervous.

"Mama, my pancake's gone. Can I have a chicken leg now?"
"After they're done, if there's one left, I'll see you
    git it.
Now go on; do real good."

The job of standing in the dining room was harder than
    Vicey had thought.
She was curious and interested at first, and craned her
    neck to see all the full plates of food.
The family ate and talked for two hours.
Vicey shifted her weight from one foot to the other.
Twice she fetched fresh napkins and once replaced a
    dropped fork.
She lost count of the platters of steaming food she
    brought from the kitchen.

When the last piece of chicken was taken off the platter,
    Vicey realized it didn't matter.
She was too tired to care.

TYING THE KNOT

*The residents on fourth floor have been saving soft
    drink cans
To tie on the wedding vehicle.
The second floor gang at Pratt Homes made crepe
    paper streamers
In the bride's colors of blue and yellow
To decorate the walls of the community room.*

*There are 85 apartments in this housing project.
All of them are rented to the elderly.
Many are widowed or divorced.
The upcoming wedding is causing great excitement,
And the atmosphere is festive.*

*Thelma and Harry have been bridge partners for years.
When Harry popped the question, Thelma said she didn't
    believe in long engagements.
The date was set for two weeks later.*

*Harry was 103 last June.
Thelma will be 87 in two days.
"Why waste time?" Harry looked at Thelma and grinned.
"I love this woman, and she loves me.
I need someone to live with, someone I love."
Thelma shook her head in agreement and slapped her
    arthritic knees as she declared,
"He kisses like heaven! We really need each other."*

*After the ceremony Harry held Thelma's hand
And kissed her on the cheek.
They rolled themselves in wheelchairs
And empty drink cans clinked behind.
Even those with failing eyesight could read
"Just Married" signs on the back of each chair.*

*The happy couple, holding hands and flirting,
Rode the elevator to the third floor.
They were looking forward to the supper
Their neighbors had arranged.
They whispered, Thelma giggled and smoothed her
    blue silk wedding dress.*

*Downstairs at the reception the soda pop punch
    and cheese straws were going quickly.
Vera and Annie Bell were saying to each other
What they'd been wondering all along,
"What in the world can those two old fools see
    in each other?
Besides, I thought Harry was interested in me."*

ON HOLD

*You called me,
  interrupting an important
    activity.*

*I answered
  and gave you full attention.
Until your phone signaled
  another call.*

*"Someone else is calling," you
  announced to me.
"Just a minute, I'll put you on hold."*

*I'd wait patiently for you to use
  the restroom
  tend to the baby
  or answer the door,
But I refuse to wait while you answer
  another call.*

The call you miss is mine.

OUR GIRL

You ought to see her now.
Four years old and a busy bundle.
She's interested in everything,
And the questions never stop.
Forget your tranquility.
There is no privacy when she's around.
She will slip your necklace on before
    breakfast,
And use your favorite nail polish to
    paint nails, knuckles and toes.

She keeps strange hours.
Falls asleep anywhere if tired,
But awakens happy and ready to play.
She changes characters before your eyes as
    she becomes a princess or waitress.
Or a stern schoolteacher giving orders to
    behave.
She's learning numbers, letters, colors
    and shapes,
But she majors in relationships.

She tags those she loves with special names:
Lee Anne becomes "Little Anne,"
Manana and Monona are her grandmothers.
She labels grandfathers, "Big-Pop," and "Other Daddy."

I like to have her visit.
She bounces on my footstool and calls me lady.
It's when she calls me "Sweet Alyce" that I
    give her anything she wants.

IS THIS THE DAY?

This may be the day
The one I've feared.
When I peep in again
There could be just a shell,
And I will face the reality I'm dreading.

This may be the last day I hold her,
Or hear the voice I've memorized.
No reason for me to be afraid.
I long for quick passage for her
Across this splintered bridge of pain.

She struggles against death,
Her suffering unrelenting.
The dependable heart rhythm is gone,
Replaced with pain and panic.
Her soft brown eyes follow me as I
     calculate dosage.
She tries not to say how bad it is,
And I hide behind the lie that all
     will be well.

I try to understand.
What she has left to give
Is the gift of sparing me.
I lean, listen, stand by.
I try to manufacture hope to replace
     our small supply.

The house is filled with death and its prelude.
The chill I feel is not related to the temperature.
I know that if she goes on even the warmest day
I will be cold.

ONE SIZE FITS ALL

It is difficult to force nylon
Over dimpled thighs
Or hung over hips.

Did hosiery designers actually
Believe one size could fit all?
Feet are one size and hips another.
Ladies tried to cope and stuff.

Now they are labeling panty hose
Petite, Average, Ample.
No one is average, and
Ample means fat!

I am taking labeling personally.
They can forget Ample, For Her Majesty,
    Queen Size and 3X-Plus.
I've bought my last pair of those
Until the hosiery company quits
Describing me.

THE AUNTS

I visited every summer with mother's sisters.
For seven days they pretended I was their child.
They were wealthy, childless and demanding.

Mother thought I enjoyed going.
I never told her I was miserable and afraid.
I didn't like their house or them
And I could tell they didn't like me.
I hated the week I spent with them.

There were several children in my family.
I thought the aunts might feel we had a child to spare.
I was afraid it might be me.
Daddy promised to come for me in one week, and
I counted the days.

Their house was filled with large mirrors, thick rugs
    and crystal chandeliers.
On the sun porch were bird cages, but I was not allowed
    to go into that room.
I could not go near their small black dog because he'd
    bite.

We ate in the large dining room.
The table was covered with a fancy tablecloth, and silver
    bowls held fresh flowers.
I worried I would spill something.
I never knew which fork to use.
Aunt Virginia warned me at each meal to be careful.
Aunt Hazel demanded I use my napkin and finger bowl.

They sat on each side of the table watching and commenting
    on my chewing and posture.
Nothing tasted good.
I pushed food around my plate and wished it was Sunday
    so I could go home.

*In the guest room I found a new toothbrush and nailbrush.
I was supposed to be well-groomed at breakfast.
If I passed inspection I was rewarded with a nickel.
If not, I was sent back to try again.
I took home few nickels.
Pleasing both of the aunts was impossible.*

*They disliked the sausage curls my mama combed.
As soon as she left, they brushed my hair into stiff braids.
"You're not pretty, Wilma," they'd say shaking their heads,
"No, you're not one bit pretty.
But we'll work hard every day you are here.
I do think we can help you become a nice young lady."*

*That's the first time I'd heard I wasn't pretty.
Mama said she had the four prettiest girls in 14 counties.
We believed her.
I knew that we were already nice.
The aunts reminded me each year that they thought I was
   ugly.
Finally, at thirteen I told Mama I didn't want to visit
   them anymore.*

*There should be something pleasant to remember
About those visits,
But I can't recall a thing.*

A SKINNY CAN'T RELATE

*Permanent skinnies don't
Collect cookbooks.
They never think whether to
Bake pies or cakes.
Certainly they don't need to diet.
They don't know what we go through.*

*Skinnies don't have three sizes of
    clothes in their closets.
They shop for skirts with pleats
And ignore A-line and dull colors.*

*Designers appeal to those who
    wear larger sizes now.
They have finally realized that
    everyone is not size four.
It's about time.*

CHANGE OF LIFE

Naomi's middle years were active and happy.
She gave little thought to growing old.
When wrinkles creased her cheeks, she ignored them.
She combed her wispy hair over the scalp's thinning spots.
When her joints stiffened, she reached for ointment,
    but she didn't count the passing years.

During her 70's she set goals before retiring.
The house she built with a neighbor's help suited
    her completely.
She dug the holes for the shrubbery
And enjoyed nailing shingles on the new roof.

Soon after the house was finished, Naomi began to feel
    lonely.
She tried not to notice that she felt uncomfortable.
Her few living friends had been moved into rest homes,
And the last of her ten brothers and sisters died.

"It's something every day," she grumbled aloud.
Nothing but aches and pains.
I seem to be someone else."
She was surprised her projects no longer mattered.
She thought anyone who napped was lazy, but she began to
    nap twice a day.
Bedtime didn't come soon enough, and she undressed long
    before dark.

Eating was a chore.
Cooking was no longer worth the trouble.
Nothing tasted good anymore.
"What is the matter with me?" she asked her mirror as
    she shuffled through the hall.
"When did I get this way?
I don't recognize myself. . . . I look like some dried-up
    stranger."

Realizing she was old shocked her deeply.
She could never find her glasses, her watch or her
    sweater.
Concentrating on TV news was difficult.
To test her memory she recited the "ABC"'s and could not
    recall what came after "K."
It seemed ridiculous that she knew which food she
    carried to a picnic forty years ago,
But could not remember what she had for breakfast.

Naomi wished she could identify the day she had become old.
"I'd have durn sure tried to prevent it," she spoke to her
    pillow.
"It must have happened while I was sleeping.
I would have refused to accept the change if I had been awake."

BE MY VALENTINE

Adjusting to a new school was difficult.
Laurie was shy and had few second grade friends
    in the new school.
The first activity she liked was making a Valentine
    box.
She was proud to be chosen to help on the decorating
    committee.
"They like me now, Mama," she explained.
"They want me to help paste red ribbons on the box."

Laurie made her own valentines.
She spent several evenings cutting hearts and
    coloring flowers.
Her teacher gave her a list of all the children's
    names,
And Laurie's mother helped with addresses.

She wore her red dress to the school party,
And was too excited to eat breakfast.
The bell was ringing when she dropped her cards
    through the slot on top of the box.
When the first valentines were given out, Laurie
    sat on the edge of her seat.

Finally she received one valentine from her teacher.
Quietly she slid back in her desk as no one called
    her name.
No one saw her put her head down; no one heard her cry.
The others were too busy opening their envelopes
    and laughing at the valentine jokes and verses.

THOMAS AT TWO MONTHS

He smiles
And makes tiny cooing sounds.
As his tiny hand
Cups my finger
I talk and sing.
His brow knits
In concentration.
"Grandmother, I love you,"
I know I heard him say it.

JANE

Jane bats her eyes and wears heavy perfume.
She is the clinging type and used to be a pretty girl.
Her conversation is sprinkled with expressions like
  "groovy," and "how cute."
The highlight of her life was being chosen homecoming
  queen in high school.
She has adored herself since that day.

Discussions of current events give her a headache.
She's more interested in arranging parties and trying
  on new clothes.
Her life revolves around twice weekly hair appointments
  with Mr. Carlos.
Lunch with the girls is her favorite pastime, and then
  she enjoys an afternoon of browsing in the stores.

I met her recently at a restaurant.
She told me of the upcoming Mrs. America Beauty Pageant.
Her eyes sparkled as she spoke of her plans to be a
  contestant.
I never saw her so thrilled.
She plans to practice a baton twirling routine and to
  learn some new dance steps.
Mr. Carlos will create a special arrangement of curls
  to hold a tiara.
Jane is having a little trouble deciding which
  costume to wear on the big night.

Twenty-five years have passed since Jane was a high
  school queen.
She needs to win this contest, and I wish her well.
I hope the judges overlook her wrinkles and neglect
  to ask difficult questions.
This trophy will see her through menopause and beyond.

ANNIE'S TREE

It was really a crepe-myrtle bush,
  but it had grown so tall it looked like a tree.
Mother admired it, and she enjoyed its lush pink
  blossoms for ten years.
Since it was her idea to light the bare branches at
  Christmastime,
We called it Annie's tree.

"It will be a good present for the neighborhood,"
  she said.
Her grandson placed ten strings of lights on the tree,
  one for each grandchild.
It was much too cold for her to go outside that first
  year,
But she watched the twinkling lights from her window.
We kept the lights on for three weeks every year, and
  it gave her more pleasure than any other gift.

The next winter was the coldest on record.
She had no strength for worrying about trees or shrubs,
  and hardly noticed the lights in the yard.
We lost Annie's tree to the bitter cold in January,
  and in Spring, we lost her too.

We decided to string the lights on the dead branches
  the next December,
To give a present to the neighborhood
In her memory.

RECOVERY ROOM

*In a strange way I float
From one wave to the next
The clock is one-handed
And I must stay
Until I can read the hour
Quarter to something will not do
I no longer care.*

*Pans clang, starched aprons rustle
A bell shatters the sterile silence
A TV drones
Someone shakes me
I am between waves and do not answer
They call insistently, bring me
Closer to pain.*

*The transfer is a void
I tremble as though outside myself
Faces appear, bodies tiptoe, no visitors
Somewhere under the cold and pain
My husband waits for me
Who is crying? (Is it me?)*

*Two thirsty days crawl by
They come in shifts to stab
The demon I sleep with.
Later, I groan more softly.
For a little while
I want to push pity
From my sister's face
Maybe tomorrow I can
Make her smile.*

NOT YOUR BASIC GARDENER

I do not understand fertilizer or mulch,
    and I don't want a green thumb.
I do not wish to converse with plants.
I don't care what kind of day they had.

No small voice beckons me to break ground
    and drop seeds in neat rows.
I haven't tried it, but I know I'd hate weeding.
Checking for mites and insects is my idea of nothing
    to do.
I know I have no talent for pruning or raking.

I believe all garden work has to be done in the
    blazing sun.
I don't want a suntan, and I don't look good in a
    straw hat.
Sweating and crawling around in the dirt doesn't
    appeal to me.
Even house plants wilt and droop in my care.
I have no idea when to water, so I drown the finest fern.

I don't know what all the fuss is about potted plants
Or why so many people want them.
I hope I'll get lucky and not get a poinsettia again
    this Christmas.

THE SPOUSE'S TOUR

The men at the convention are learning about
    tax reform
And current marketing strategy.
They are exchanging "good 'ol boy" stories,
    and are having a wonderful time.

Another delightful afternoon has been planned for
    the ladies.
The object is to keep us occupied and happy.
Perhaps someone thinks a hot bus ride to nowhere
    is fun,
And maybe some would enjoy a ride through the
    Everglades.

I am not forced to go on this tour.
I could choose to remain at the hotel and play
    solitaire
And be thought antisocial.
Today we will visit Miss Ellie's Southfork Ranch.
I want to see if they sell as souvenirs
    squares of soil J.R. Ewing walked on.
Surely no one pays for a dirt sample.

We are jammed in a bus.
The air-conditioning quits as it did last time.
This ranch is 65 miles away and patience is thin.
We tour Southfork; the ranch is a fake.
There is an ordinary farm house with a children's pool.
Everyone clamors back on the bus, disappointed.
There is one happy lady who clutches her soil sample
    and passes it around.

They can join the spouse's tour next year if they like.
I've done my time.

BUD

No one knew Bud's last name.
In fact, no one ever knew Bud.
He slept in the park when the weather was warm.
During the winter he curled up in a discarded
 appliance box
And slept under the library stairs.
City officials insisted he move when they discovered
 a few empty wine bottles.
People considered him a disgrace.

He was shabby and smelly.
He wouldn't take a job, but pleasantly declined.
He walked from the depot to the fairgrounds every
 day
And tipped his cap to those he passed, and smiled his
 toothless grin.
Pets and children followed him.
They didn't care that his jacket was worn or that
 his shoes were stained.
He whistled as if he were happy.
I don't know how he could have been because he wasn't
 welcome in town.
He didn't seem to notice.

No one knew how he managed, but he didn't steal.
He turned in a lost wallet and hat to the police
 department last year.
Recently he was found unconscious on a bench in the park.
They think he had a stroke.
It took several hours to count all the $20 bills
 in his jacket and shoes.

Everyone in town has an opinion about
    the cash.
The golf course needs a sprinkler, and they want
    concrete planters for the mall.
They argued two hours about buying things for the
    town before someone remembered Bud.

A motion was made that a marble marker be erected
    at his grave.
There would still be money for civic projects.
The crowd grew silent, and the motion died for lack
    of a second.
I hope Bud was happy living in this town.
I don't like it here as well as I did before.

THE FITTING

When I shopped for a mother-of-the-groom dress,
High school girls were selecting prom dresses.
The fitting room was filled with giggling girls,
And the alterations lady was doing her best
    to fit them as they twisted and twirled.

I shared a dressing room with four girls in
    bikini underwear.
I felt old and dowdy.
My dress looked dull and ordinary beside glittering
Colors of electric blue, pink satin and yellow.

I walked to the full-length mirror.
The young ladies could not hide their shock.
One of them whispered to her friend,
"Where do you think she's going in that?"
They rolled their eyes heavenward.
My dress probably looked like a mauve pillowcase
    to them.
But I was happy not to be struggling with a strapless
    top.

I found a box to sit on and invited all of them to
    be fitted first.
I'd rather wait than have them stare.
I had forgotten what teen-aged girls worry about.
One said, "I hope he doesn't bring me a pink corsage;
    I mean really I'll just die!"
None of them could imagine they would ever need to
    buy a dress like mine.
They will.

BEFORE THE FUNERAL

*The den is crowded with relatives talking about
     this and that . . .
Little groups enjoying aimless conversation
As though silence would be unwelcome on this day.*

*I have no interest in Aunt Sudie's visit,
Or in the new wine you tasted on your trip.
"Life goes on," I'm told with exaggerated gentleness.
No, it doesn't. Not today. It stops.
It does not know the way to continue so quickly.*

*I cannot measure the emptiness I have.
It is a void, so fresh, so real it blinds me.
There are not enough tears to fill it
If the whole world was crying.*

*They eat, drink, shake hands and brush the
     crumbs away,
As though it were a picnic.
They wipe their mouths with napkins, not their eyes.
Isn't that curious? I move around the circus and
     observe a game.*

*Please don't ask me to join your group.
And do not tell me when I'm hungry,
Or that you think it's time for us to go.*

THE BANQUET SPEAKER

I'm trying to pay attention,
But I am not entertained.
He's been talking thirty minutes.
This chair is getting hard.

I shouldn't have eaten the dressing
Or those hard, green peas.
People have begun to nod,
And the hot coffee is gone.

I don't think he has a point.
He could ramble on an hour
Trying to be witty.
He's having a wonderful time,
But no one laughed at the last joke.

He's through?
Everyone is standing, clapping.
Glad to know they can go home
And quit being polite.

THE LINEN CLOSET

When we first built the house
And the closets were new
I had shelves built for linen
And I labeled them too.

Twin sheets and towels
Had a place of their own
Bath mats and pillows
Were stacked all alone.

It was all very simple
One thing had me beat
I never learned how
To fold a fitted sheet.

I tried matching corners
And folded them then
They seemed to grow bigger
So I soon stuffed them in.

So, here's to the closets
All magazines show
Shelves covered with scented
Shelf paper, just so.

If you open my closet
There won't be a doubt
You'll know which sheets are fitted
As they all tumble out.

THE INSTRUCTOR

*During exercise class Miss Perry wore black cotton
    bloomers.*
I thought she looked like a prune.
*She taught science and physical education and meant
    business.*
No fun or nonsense for me in eighth grade.

Our exercise instruction was organized and difficult.
There were rules for everything.
She insisted things be done right the first time.
*She was fair; she enforced the rules; her punishment
    was certain.*

I never saw a lady so dedicated to physical activity.
*She ordered us to run fast, jump high and bend
    correctly.*
I was lazy and had no interest in sports.
I preferred to draw pictures.
Josephine Perry was not interested in art.

*She called running laps around the ball field
    "warm-up time."*
If you lagged behind, she blew her whistle.
If she had to blow it twice, extra laps were in order.
Grumbling and complaining were not tolerated.
*"Run faster," she commanded as I limped around
    the track.*
I had to run extra laps every day.

I never learned to do push-ups or jumping jacks.
I couldn't do deep knee bends or play softball.
*"Fitness is important," she'd swish her long gray
    ponytail*
And we giggled and made fun of her.

Now, in my fifties I know she was right.
I'd like to run a lap with her and tell her so.

THE SHOPPING TRIP

*At the drugstore
She peers at the labels
And tries to read the fine print
Through thick cataract glasses.*

*She moves slowly
Up and down the aisles
Hoping she won't forget
What she needs most.*

*Her children advised her
To make a list.
"Write it down," they insist.
She said, "I don't want my brains on paper,"
Insulted that they had suggested a crutch.*

*"Where would I be if I lost the list?"
She hesitates to ask for help
Other shoppers might think she is dumb.
So she tries harder each week to remember
Denture creme, laxative and snuff
And lollipops for the grandchildren.*

VISITING

Thomas is spending the day with me.
    I will show him the baby robins
    And the new red geraniums.
    We need to talk about important things
    And to smile and touch.

We will sing patty-cake songs
    And read about the cow that jumped over the moon.
    All his smiles will be for me,
    And I've saved up hugs for him.

He will fill the house again
    With baby sounds and laughter.
    Every corner will smell sweeter,
    And my rocking chair is ready to hold him.

Thomas is spending the day with me.
    I hope there are no phone calls
    No unexpected visitors to entertain.
    I have no time for anyone else today.
    I may stand and watch him while he sleeps.
    He isn't going to be a baby long.

THE SWIMMING LESSON

I hung on to the side of the pool for a week.
Why did I sign up for swimming?

My contact with the water was casual,
And I was determined not to get my face wet.

Near the middle of the pool I faked it
And paddled my hands as I stood firmly on the bottom.

Then the instructor got serious.
He invited us to swim past him alone
And I dog-paddled, head high.

"You," he singled me out,
"You are not *swimming."*

He pushed my head under, and I came up sputtering.
I thought of charging assault.

Seven days went by, and I made no progress.
To graduate we had to dive into eight feet of water.

I dove.
It took three rescue workers to clear my lungs.
I was asked to repeat the class.

They must be kidding.
I'm never going to go near water again.

NEW MOTHER

And did you really think he'd care?
The shock was too much.
The pleasure of the moment recalled.
He gave no thought to this predicament
Then or now.

"A baby?
What is that to me?" he said.
"You know there have been others.
I've got football practice,
And we run track at three."

Already you are morning sick
And swollen and alone.
Your mother guesses
But doesn't face the truth.
Your daddy is worried that you do not play
Anymore.

You should be dressing for the prom
And cheering for the team.
You should be buying earrings and makeup.
Instead you hide stolen diapers
Under your bed
And weep.

ANY NEWS?

Among the dry cleaner stubs
I found the note today
I was never meant to see.
A few loving words have changed my life
And trust is gone.

You whistle as before
Try to kiss me as you pass the stove.
"Any news?" you ask
As you go through the mail.
I have no interest in world affairs tonight.
There will be no small talk to fill the silence.

I serve our plates and search your face
I could inquire with casual words
What difference will your answer make?
Yes will reinforce the truth I know
No will be another lie I can despise
As well as her.

How quickly I've forgotten
When I was calm and knew you loved me
When I drew closer as you spoke
Or smiled at the sight of you
Coming up the walk.
You will probably blush
And stammer when I tell you
Yes, there is news.
The game is over.

WHERE HAS THE TIME GONE?

*Where has the time gone
Since I met you
And loved you instantly.*

*The busy years hurried by
We knew instinctively
That trust was ours.*

*Now, the changes are incredible
Hair is white
Shoulders stooped
Steps slower.*

*The years melted quickly
Into each other
One thing is still the same
I've always loved you
And I always will.*

CLEAN UP

*Brown sticks litter the deck
Blown free by yesterday's storm.
I toss them away
Paying little attention.
One moves, a snake twists
And flops over my wrist.
I shake it loose
And scream
And watch it slither away
My relaxing afternoons
On the deck are over
And I wonder if snakes
Are able to crawl into the house.*

THE FEMALE

She doesn't fly
Just flashes to attract.
A tiny pulse of light
To let him know
On which branch she waits.
She calls him
In lightning bug language
Hoping he'll flash back
And visit for awhile.

WHEN I GO

Beloved, when I go
Sing me your gayest song
And speak of all
The happy times we knew

Remember how we loved
Forget the rest
And I shall wait
Impatiently for you.

BUSYBODY

Move the tray on the coffee table
The books beside the chair
Get rid of lamp cords and dishes
He's walking everywhere.

We follow to prevent tumbles
His eye is bruised from a fall
If the phone rings forget it
He might try the stairs in the hall.

No small speck escapes his notice
He follows an ant on the floor
He lifts tiny arms for balance
We smile, clap and beg for more.

He's the center of attention
He explores each table and chair
We encourage, guard, adore him
Sweet Thomas is everywhere.

RETIREMENT

We always got along so well
For 37 years we knew routine.
On Sunday nights he yawned and said,
"Tomorrow is another workday."
He smiled when he made this announcement.
Each day he dressed and went to work.
I went about my own business.

He is retired now.
I am busier than ever.
My life is upside down.
I am not used to supervision and
    second opinions.
He asks, "Why don't you do it this way?
      Where are you going now?
      When will you be back?
      Who was on the phone?
      What are we having for dinner?"

He follows me from room to room
Leaving a trail of papers, socks and ashes.
He doesn't see the overflowing trash
As he reaches for another cookie.

He opens the refrigerator forty times a day.
"I don't know what I want," he sighs.
After a long look at tomatoes and leftovers
He repeats, "I just don't know what I want."

I know what I want.
(Could you please get another job
    and go to work?)

THE CEMETERY

There is a dull conformity in this place
Policy dictates the height of grass
Flat stone markers designate the spot where
    bodies lie
The uniformity may be comforting to some
But she loved individuality.

I wish buttercups could bloom nearby
And that crabapple trees
    were where she lies.
I remember the one she treasured in her yard.

Just one tree. What could it hurt?
This cemetery would seem less sad.

ONE DAY AT A TIME

DAY 1

A neighbor's child shouted at my window,
"Your boy's been hit by a car!"
I ran the half block to take Mark from a stranger.
Someone was guiding his twisted bicycle.
We told him at five that he was a big boy.
Now it is not so.
He is small, pale and hurt.
In the emergency room they find bruises and send
    us home.
Long after Mark was calm and playing, I continued
    to shake
And pray with thanksgiving.

DAY 2

The bicycle was put in storage.
He outgrew his tricycle a year ago, but that is
    all he had permission to ride.
Mark's blonde curls were beautiful in the sun,
And I was pouring a cup of coffee when he screamed.
The tricycle jack knifed, and he was thrown against
    the concrete.
Gentle hands stitched his face in the emergency room.
He is proud of his bandage and balloon
And they tell him what a brave boy he is.
They suggest I take a sedative.

DAY 3

Mark begged to play on the patio.
No wheels of any kind today.
A little frog was near the steps so I let him go.
Few moments passed before I heard the crash.
He had dropped the jar he found for the frog's home.
The jagged glass ripped his arm and hand.
The towels I wrapped around his arm were bloody
    when we reached the hospital.
We were both crying, and they didn't need to ask
    our names.
Again they hugged Mark and gave him more balloons
    and stitches.
They just looked at me and shook their heads.

WHEN I AM OLD

*I shall wear bright colors
When I am old
Hot pinks and purples and
Stripes of red as it suits me.
No more neutral shades for
Practicality.*

*I will be on no schedule
And will go where I've never been
When I take a notion.
There is no reason I should not go
    to Alaska, Hong Kong, wherever.
And come back when I please.*

*I will read till three a.m.
And cook rare steak for breakfast.
I will disconnect the phone when
I am busy painting a new picture.*

*I will give beloved things away
While I can have the pleasure
    of seeing the gift received.
I will have no need for collections
When I am old.*

EASTER BONNET

It's impossible to guess what kind of hats
    will attract ladies.
Mrs. Skinny will want a huge cartwheel with
    net cabbage roses.
Madame Fats will prefer a pillbox hat
    perched above her double chins.

I sold hats one Easter and saw the ugliest
    ones find buyers.
It helped when I commented, "This hat was
    made for you."
Occasionally a customer would question,
"Are you sure?
Do you really think this hat is becoming?"

I was trained to say,
"My dear, it's gorgeous!
It's really YOU."

BROTHER RON AND SISTER PHYLLIS

The Hallelujah Jubilee Hour is on TV again.
It blesses some and is entertainment for others.
I'm tired of nonstop begging and pleading for money.
I wonder why they don't plan their projects according
 to the funds they have.

Brother Ron says large donations mean a special
 blessing,
And he encourages people to give.
"Make a commitment, honor your pledge," he begs for
 a monthly pledge
To underwrite future projects.
His eyes mist, his chin trembles, and he describes what
 a rough year it has been.
His Mercedes payment is due.

They offer gifts if you double your donation.
Plans are ambitious.
Brother Ron is developing motels
 for all who visit.
He prefers a live audience.
The collection plate is passed between each of Phyllis'
 songs.

In spite of Ron's huge salary and Phyllis' income from
 records and tapes,
They are fretting that their condominium is unfinished.
Phyllis' Cadillac is two years old and needs to be
 replaced.
Wouldn't look right if she drove a Pinto.

*It's time to plan their annual cruise
    to the Mediterranean.
Ron's last sermon was titled, "No Need for a Christian
    to Be Poor."
When he'd made his point, the phones lit up,
    and the pledges set a record.
Bank employees stood by to safeguard the offering.*

*Phyllis gets emotional about finances, rolls her eyes,
    lifts her arms heavenward,
And says she wouldn't want any other job in the world.
I guess not. No other job would ever pay as well.
She is going to the Orient for six weeks,
Then to Hawaii for a month of rest.
She can afford it.*

*Brother Ron will escort her and hopes to set up new
    satellite stations
For extensive TV coverage.
He will sign autographs for his new book,*
Give, without Counting the Cost.

*Be a shame for these two soul-winners to have a simple
    pastorate,
Where they would preach on Sunday without makeup or
    microphones,
Or visit the sick or imprisoned.
Be a pity not to make use of their talent for promotion
    and show business.*

*My neighbor sends most of her
    social security check
Whether she buys food* or *medicine.
Once in awhile she gets a form letter from Brother Ron
    telling her the Lord loves her
And she is special.*

NATURE'S GIFT

Fat white flakes of snow
*   Beginning to stick*
*   On the brick wall*
A present for everyone
*   This Christmas Eve.*

PHOTO

*I relax while they
Adjust the lights
   and focus.*

*When they stand beside
The camera to shoot
And advise me to, "say cheese,"
I freeze.*

DAUGHTERS, FINALLY

The men have left the table
Sunday dinner at Mama's.
They rush to shoot baskets
Watch the Redskins game
Take a snooze.

I visit with my son's wives
Daughters, finally.
We enjoy girl talk
Nice to have the company
Of these blue-eyed girls
My sons and I adore.

OLD FRIEND

The basketball net hangs loosely
On the rim of the hoop
Torn and frayed
Waiting for the boys
To come home and shoot a few.

GOODNIGHT

I make the coffee
He locks the doors
Two kisses
One expected
The second one for love.

SEPTEMBER MORNING

We sat together each September
Watching the first school bus
 stop for the children.
When our last boys climbed aboard
We were proud but sad.

Remember how we promised
To observe this ritual every year
Even when we were old ladies
Drinking hot coffee on the porch
And drawing our jackets closer
Against the chill?

I still watch for the bus
And smile at the new jeans
And eager fresh-washed faces.
I sit alone
Now that you are gone
And keep the ritual in your memory.

COMFORT

*High heels, sling backs
Patent leather sandals
Pinch and torture me
    after 30 minutes.*

*Wedge heels keep me off balance
Pumps with pointed toes make
    my feet cramp.
Often now I sacrifice beauty
    and style
And reach for tennis shoes.*

DAY PEOPLE

*They're the ones who ring your phone
    at 7:30 a.m.
Surprised you aren't awake.
They rise fresh and whistling
And consider the rest of us lazy.*

*They babble about sunlight
And songbirds
And enjoy early morning jogs.
They think it's OK to mow lawns
    at dawn.*

*They'll tell you about the fresh air
    and the dew
But they have no idea how wonderful
    midnight is.
Don't count on them doing anything
    productive in the evening.
They fold after the seven o'clock news.*